My Visit to the AIRPORT

Diana Bentley
Reading Consultant
University of Reading

Photographs by
Paul Seheult

My Visit

My Visit to the Airport
My Visit to the Birthday Party
My Visit to the Dentist
My Visit to the Doctor
My Visit to the Hospital
My Visit to the Seaside
My Visit to the Supermarket
My Visit to the Swimming Baths
My Visit to the Zoo

First Published in 1989 by
Wayland (Publishers) Limited
61 Western Road, Hove
East Sussex, BN3 1JD, England

© Copyright 1989 Wayland (Publishers) Limited

Editor: Sophie Davies

British Library Cataloguing in Publication Data

Bentley , Diana
  My visit to the airport.
  1. English language reader. - For children
  I. Title II. Seheult, Paul
  428.6

ISBN 1 85210 714 6

Typeset by: Lizzie George, Wayland
Printed and bound by Casterman S.A., Belgium

Contents

All words that appear in **bold** are explained in the glossary on page 22.

Hello, my name is Alex.

Today Mum and I are going to the airport.
We are going to meet our friend Claire. We
are taking the train to the airport. Mum buys
the tickets at the station. I give my ticket to
the guard.

We take the train to the airport.

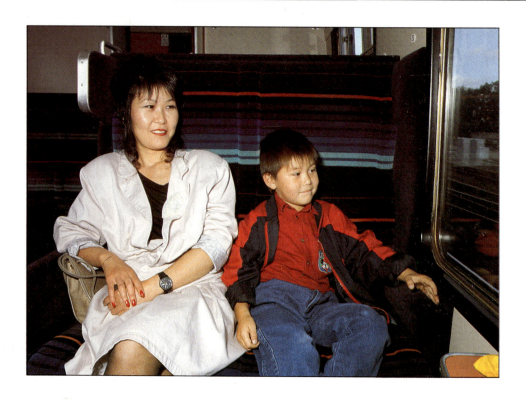

Now we are on the train. I look out of the window. I can see the aeroplanes so we must be near.

We don't have to walk to the airport. We can use the **moving walkway**. We stand still and the walkway carries us along.

The airport is very busy.

Look at the crowds! This is the check-in desk.
The **passengers** show their tickets at the
desk. They leave their bags here too.

These people tell the passengers where to go to catch their aeroplane.

An aeroplane is landing.

I sit by the window and look at the
aeroplanes. It is very busy outside. Lorries
and vans drive to and from the aeroplanes.
Some people are cleaning the aeroplanes.

Some people are putting the luggage and the food on board. Look, an aeroplane is going to land. It flies towards the **runway**. It lands on the runway and slows down until it stops. Now the passengers can get out.

There are lots of shops and cafés at the airport.

We go to the teddy bear shop. My Granny gave me some money for my birthday. Mum says I can spend it on a toy. I choose a furry puppet. I am very lucky! Then we go to a café. I have a sandwich for my lunch.

We go on to the balcony to look at aeroplanes.

This is where people come to look at aeroplanes. There is a **telescope** so you can see more clearly. I put in a coin, and Mum lifts me up so I can look. I see aeroplanes from lots of different countries.

Now it is nearly time to meet Claire. This screen tells us that her flight has landed.

Claire finds her suitcase.

This is called a **baggage carousel**. The bags go round and round. Claire sees her suitcase, and picks it up. Now she must show her **passport**, and go through **Customs**.

The Customs people check that no one has anything in their bags that is not allowed. Claire comes to look for us.

Here comes Claire at last!

I can see Claire coming through the doors.
Mum and I wave to her. We are very happy
to see her again. I run to give her a big hug.

Now we are on our way home.

Now we are back in our home town. Claire is tired, so Mum carries her suitcase. I have had a very exciting day at the airport. Now I am going home with my new puppet. Goodbye!

Glossary

Baggage carousel   The place where you collect your bags after a flight.

Customs   Here, people may check your bags when you arrive in a country. They make sure you don't bring in anything that is not allowed.

Moving walkway   A part of the floor that carries you along. It helps people who have heavy bags.

Passengers   People who travel by aeroplane, ship, train or bus.

Passport   A book that says who you are and where you are from. It has a photograph of you inside. You need it to go from one country to another.

Runway   A long wide road at an airport. Aeroplanes go down it when they take off and land.

Telescope A long tube that makes faraway things look nearer.

Books to read

Airports Graham Rickard (Wayland, 1986)
Build Your Own Airport Caroline Pitcher
  (Franklin Watts, 1987)
Let's Look at Aircraft Andrew Langley
  (Wayland, 1989)
On a Plane Jenny Vaughan (Franklin Watts,
  1987)

Acknowledgements

The author and publishers would like to thank Yoshi and Alexander Williams; Cynthia Roberts; and the staff at Gatwick Airport, for their help with this book.
The picture on page 11 is from Zefa.

Index

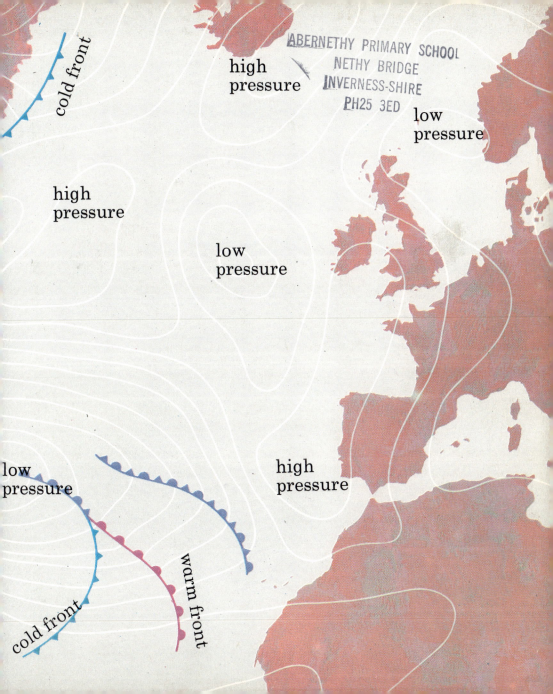

First published in 1971 by
Macdonald Educational
St Giles House
49 Poland Street
London W1

Chief Editor
Angela Sheehan B.A.

© Macdonald and Company
(Publishers) 1971
3rd impression 1975
ISBN 0 356 03673 1
MFL 25

Made and printed in Great Britain
by A. Wheaton & Company
Exeter Devon